PIANO  SOLO

KEEP
CALM
AND
PLAY
ON

WISE PUBLICATIONS
part of The Music Sales Group

London / New York / Paris / Sydney / Copenhagen / Berlin / Madrid / Hong Kong / Tokyo

Published by
WISE PUBLICATIONS
14-15 Berners Street, London W1T 3LJ,
United Kingdom.

Exclusive Distributors:
MUSIC SALES LIMITED
Distribution Centre, Newmarket Road,
Bury St Edmunds, Suffolk IP33 3YB,
United Kingdom.
MUSIC SALES PTY LIMITED
20 Resolution Drive, Caringbah, NSW 2229,
Australia.

Order No. AM1005037
ISBN 978-1-78038-655-3
This book © Copyright 2012 Wise Publications,
a division of Music Sales Limited.

Edited by Jenni Norey.
Cover designed by Michael Bell Design.
Printed in the EU.

www.musicsales.com

6/11/98

Music by Joby Talbot.

ALEXANDRA PARK

Composed by John Metcalfe.

THE ART OF FLYING

Music by Zbigniew Preisner.

Back home again, returning to life, same turmoil, phones, faxes?...
Just true life. Or the art of flying.

18

20

BIG MY SECRET

(FROM THE PIANO)

Music by Michael Nyman.

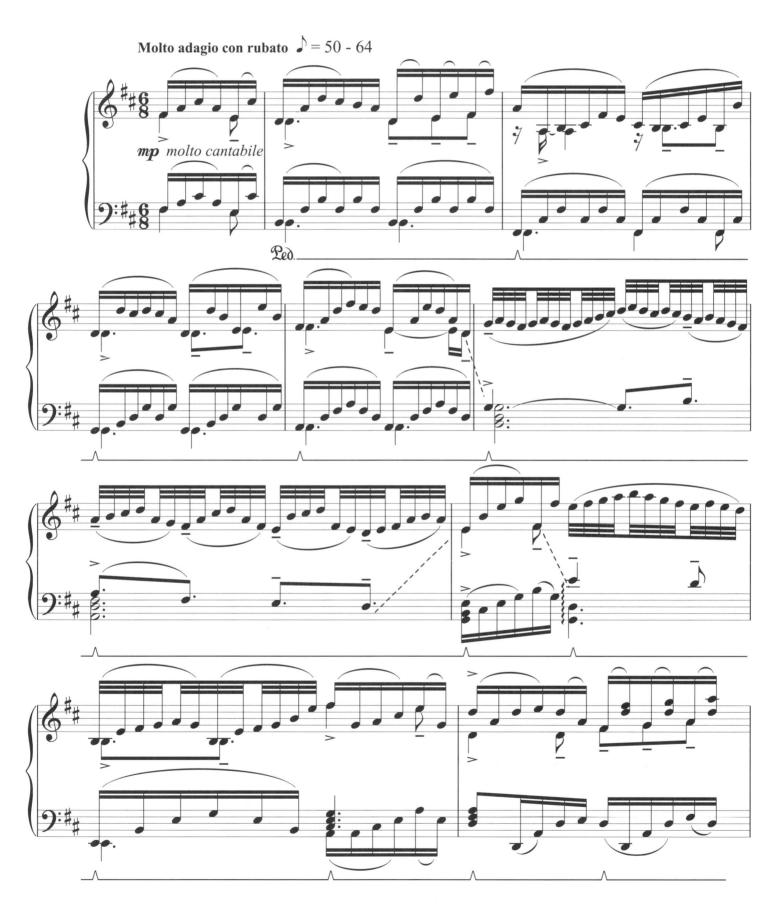

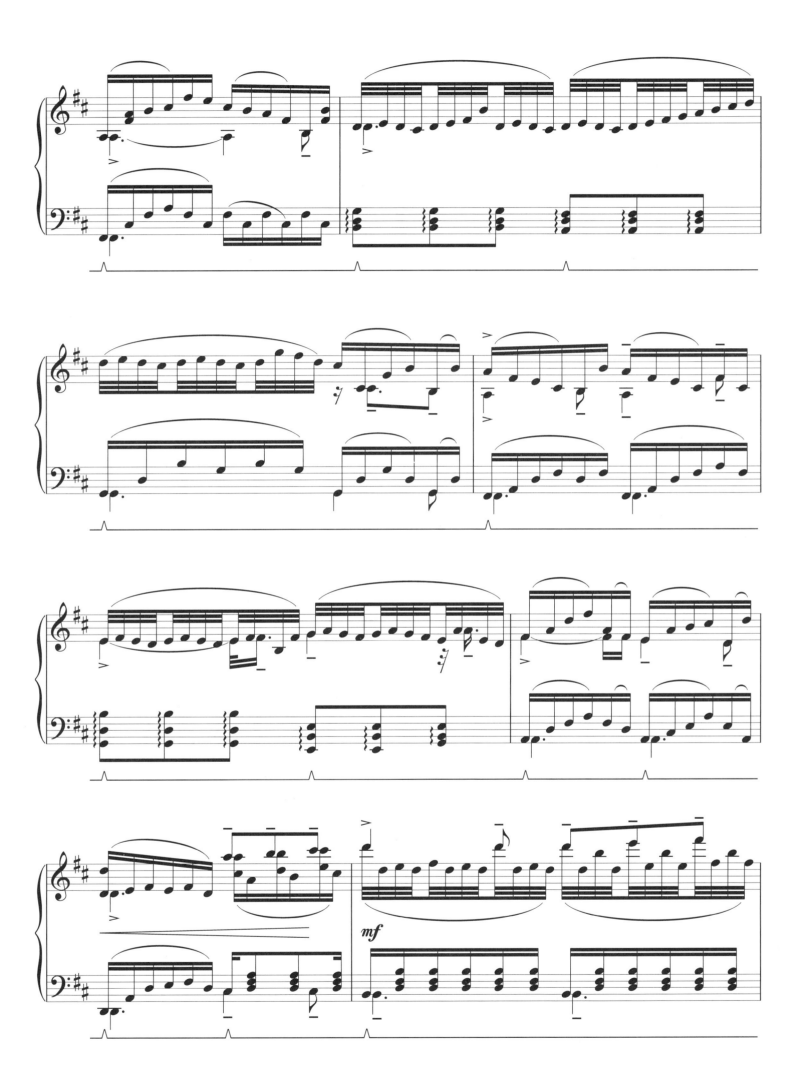

CANDLEFIRE

(FROM THE DIARY OF ANNE FRANK)

Music by Michael Nyman.

♩ = c.60

COMME UNE ROSÉE DE LARMES

(FROM THE ARTIST)

Music by Ludovic Bource.

CLOSE COVER

Music by Wim Mertens.

COMPTINE D'UN AUTRE ETÉ

(FROM AMÉLIE)

Words & Music by Yann Tiersen.

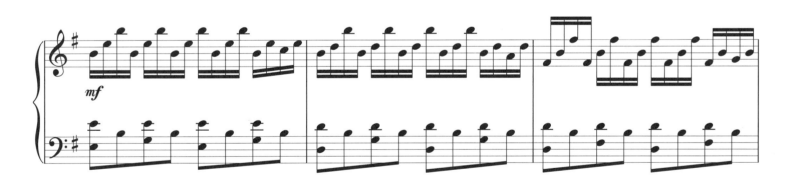

DIVENIRE

Music by Ludovico Einaudi.

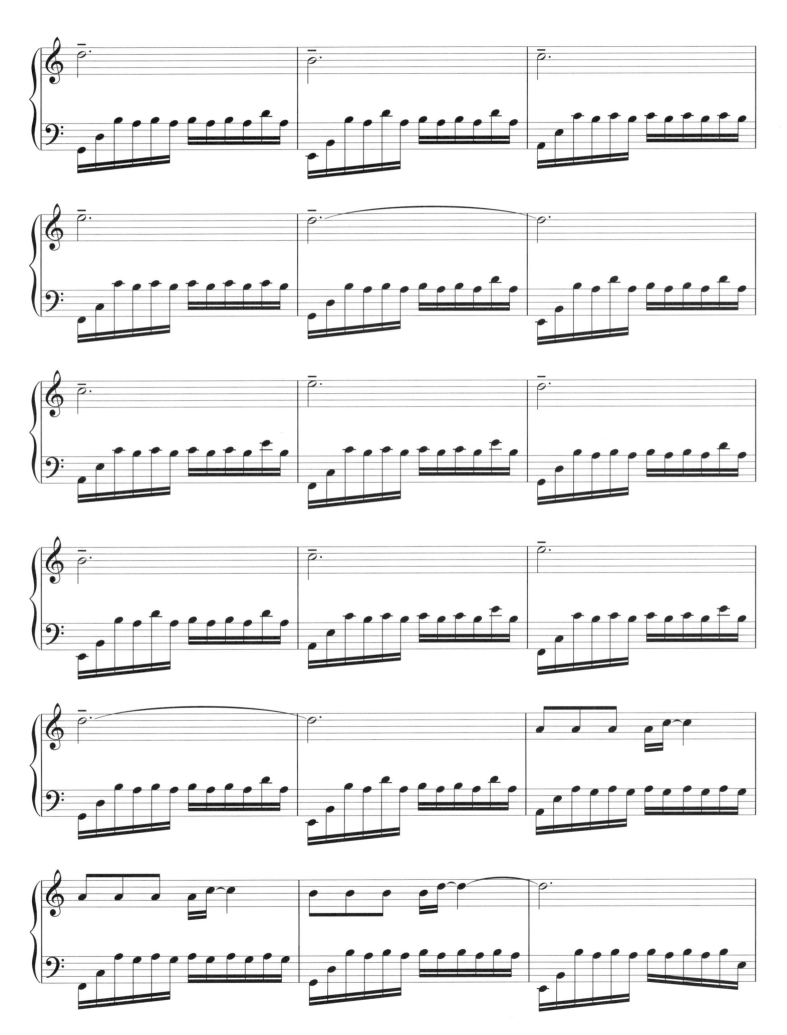

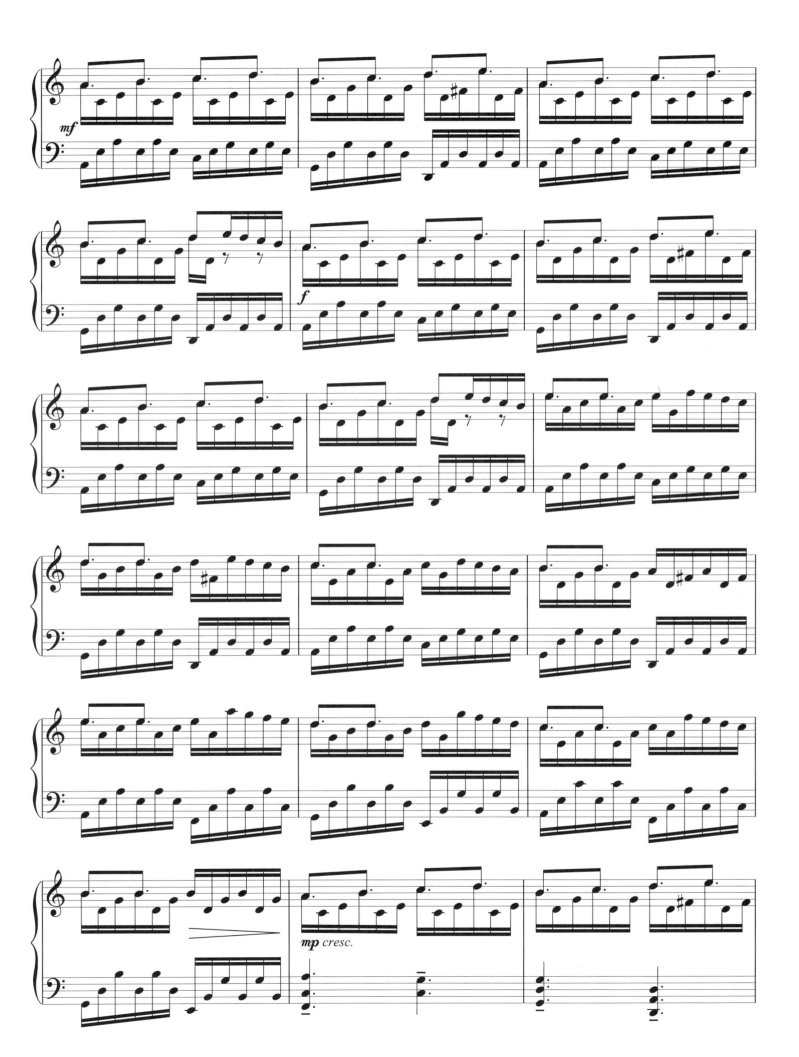

ERLA'S WALTZ

Music by Ólafur Arnalds.

EUSTACE AND HILDA

(FROM THE BBC TV PRODUCTION EUSTACE AND HILDA)

Music by Sir Richard Rodney Bennett.

FAREWELL

Music by Zbigniew Preisner.

poco a poco cresc.

rit.

mf

FLY

Music by Ludovico Einaudi.

Piano sample
and electronic
effects cont.
and fade.

GRACEFUL GHOST

Words & Music by William Bolcom.

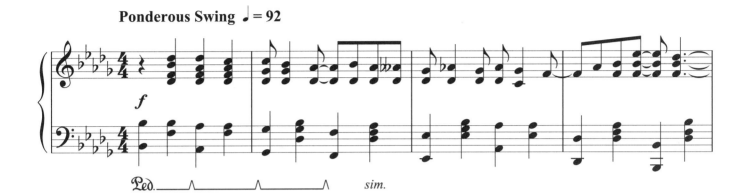

rall.

a tempo poco meno mosso ♩ = 82

Rubato (straight 8ths)　　　　**Tempo I (Swing 8ths)**　　**poco rall.**

(very long pause)

HUSH

Composed by Craig Armstrong.

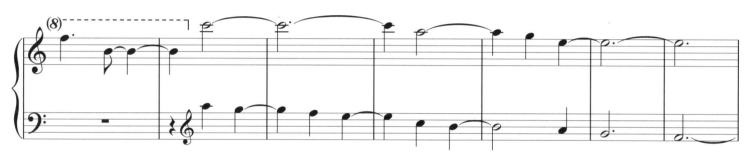

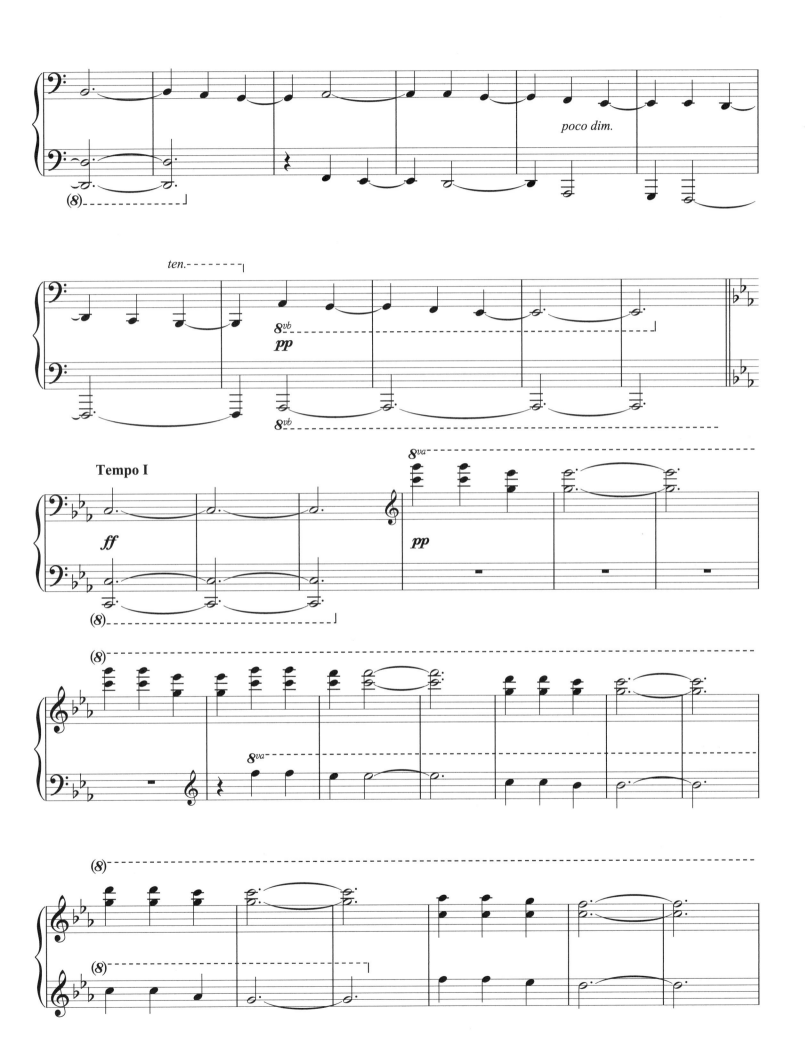

THE KING'S SPEECH

Music by Alexandre Desplat.

KISS THE RAIN

Music by Yiruma.

OPENING
(FROM GLASSWORKS)

Composed by Philip Glass.

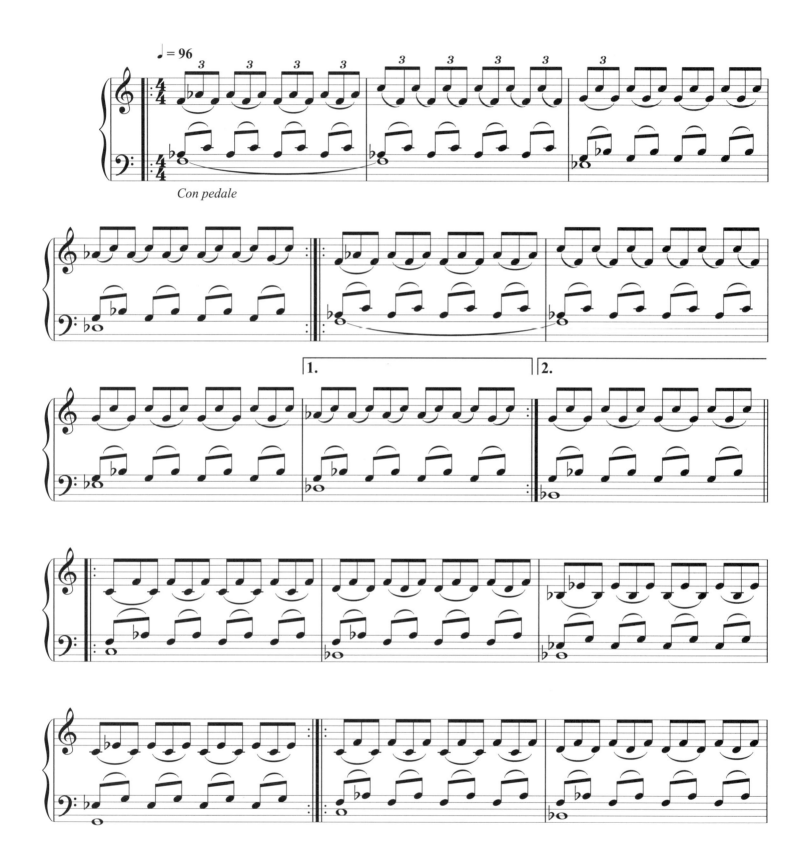

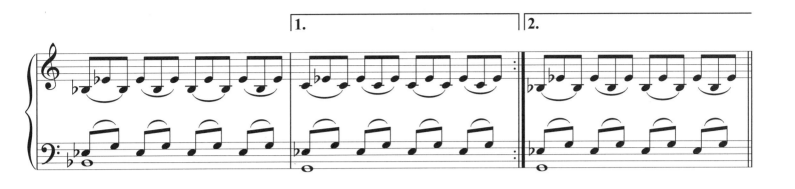

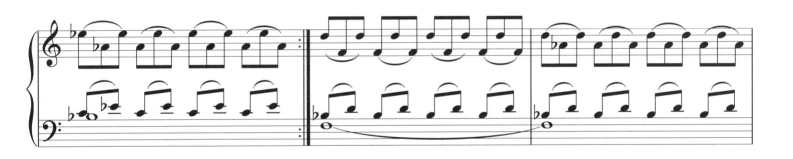

D.C. twice

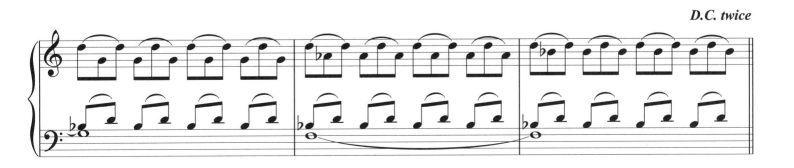

PRELUDE NO. 2

Composed by Dustin O'Halloran.

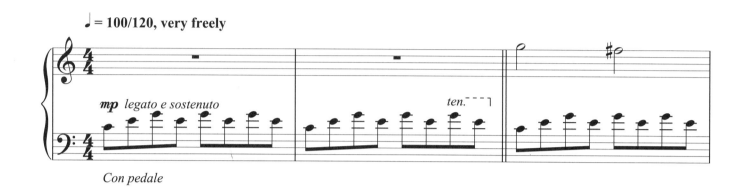

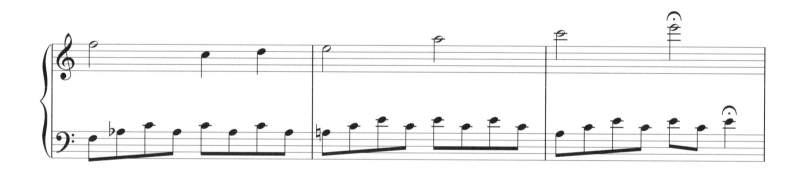

RIVER FLOWS IN YOU

Music by Yiruma.

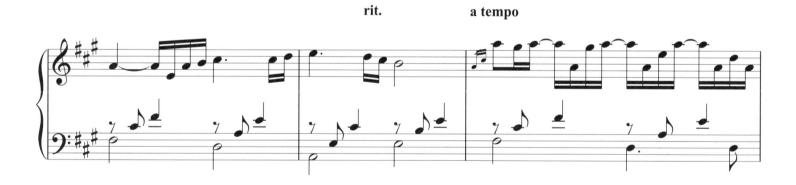

ROMANCE

(FROM SYLVIA)

Music by Gabriel Yared.

TREASURE

Music by Alberto Iglesias.

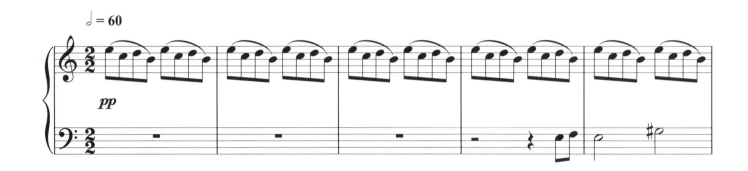

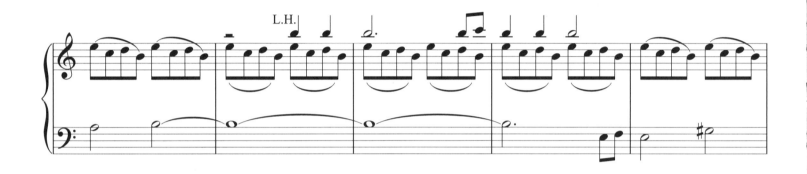

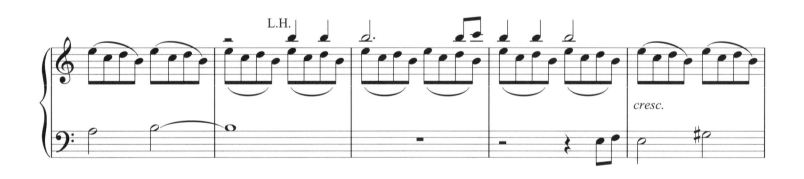

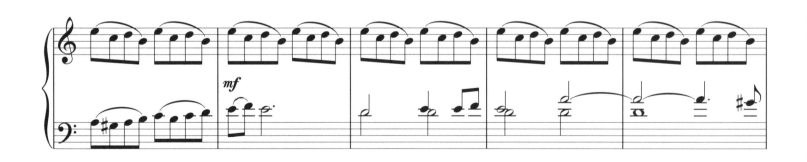